The Arctic and the Antarctic
Polar Opposites

Foundations Level D Readers

Printed in the United States of America.

Royalty Free Images: Shutterstock

Logic of English, Inc
4865 19th Street NW, Suite 130
Rochester, MN 55901

ISBN 978-1-936706-17-4
First Edition
10 9 8 7 6 5 4

Denise Eide

www.LogicofEnglish.com

The Earth is shaped like a **sphere** or a ball. At the top is the North Pole. The area around the North Pole is called the Arctic.

At the bottom is the South Pole. The area around the South Pole is called the Antarctic. *Ant-* means opposite. The Arctic and the Antarctic are polar opposites.

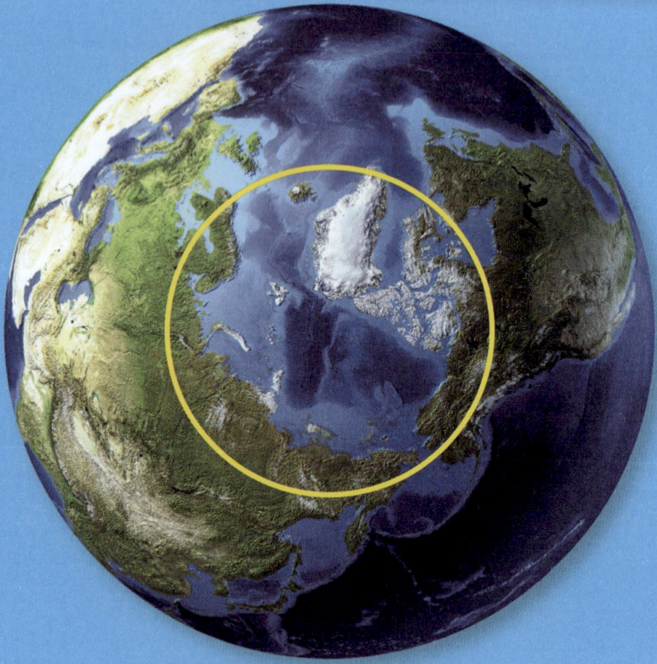

Water surrounded by land

The Arctic is a circular area with water in the middle and land around it. Because it is so cold, the water freezes into ice. The water is called the Arctic Ocean.

Chuckchi

Inuit

Arctic houses

Thousands of years ago, humans walked north from the lands surrounding the Arctic. They built houses and made the Arctic their home.

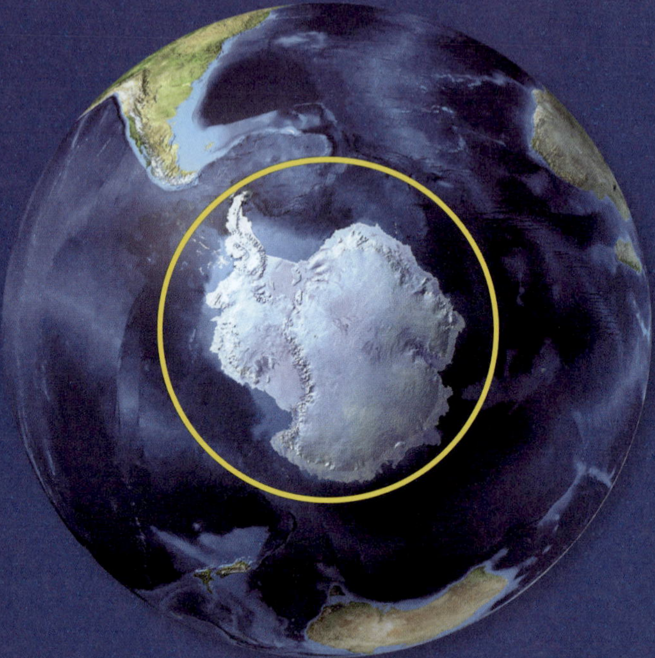

Land surrounded by water

The Antarctic is land surrounded by water. The land is called Antarctica. Because Antarctica is separated from other lands, no one could walk to it.

Antarctica

James Cook was the first to sail the Antarctic Ocean in 1773, but he did not go far enough to see Antarctica. The land was first seen in 1820. Today, researchers and tourists visit the Antarctic, but no one lives there.

Flowers blooming in snow

Winter tundra with small plants

The Arctic has cold winters with lots of snow. It can be as cold as -58° F. In the winter, snow falls and covers the ground. The Arctic has short, cool summers.

Arctic tundra in summer

In some places the snow melts in the summer. Small plants and grasses cover the ground. But the summer is too short for trees to grow. Land where it is too cold for trees to grow is called **tundra**.

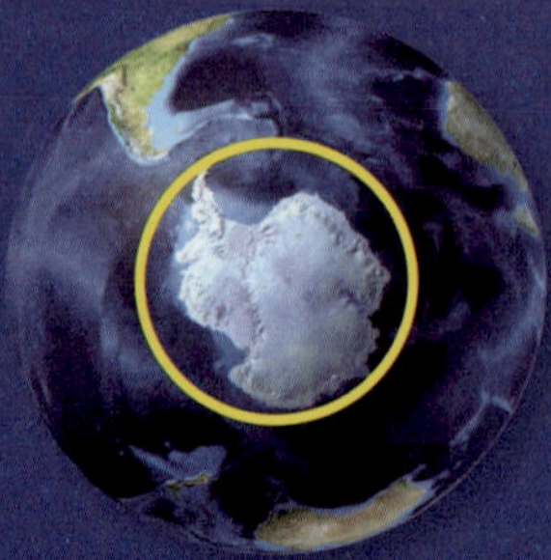

Antarctica

Antarctica

The Antarctic is the coldest place on earth. In winter it can be as cold as -128° F. It rarely snows in the Antarctic. However, in most of the Antarctic the snow that does fall never melts.

A frozen desert

Much of the Antarctic is a frozen **desert**. A desert is a place with little rain or snow. No plants grow on Antarctica.

Killer Whales

Polar Bears

Walrus

Many kinds of animals live in the Arctic. The Arctic Ocean is filled with whales and fish. Many animals, such as polar bears, seals, and walruses, live on land and hunt in the ocean.

Arctic Fox

Arctic Hare

Snowy Owl

Reindeer

In the tundra some animals, such as hares and reindeer, eat the plants. Other land animals, such as foxes and owls, hunt for smaller animals. Polar bears live only in the Arctic.

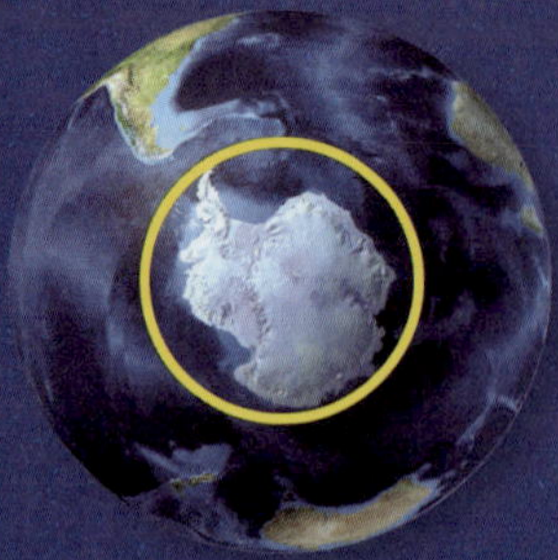

King Penguin

Elephant Seal

Whale

Because there are no plants to eat on Antarctica, there are no land animals. All the animals in the Antarctic live in or next to the ocean. They find all their food in the water.

Emperor Penguin

Whales, birds, and seals live in the ocean around Antarctica. Penguins live in the Antarctic too.

Antarctic

Arctic

Though the Arctic and the Antarctic are both cold and full of ice, they are very different places.

Tundra in the summer in the Arctic

Caribou in the Arctic

The Arctic is water surrounded by land. It snows often in the Arctic. The land in the Arctic is tundra, and plants and land animals live there.

Paradise Bay in Antarctica

Penguins live near the water in the Antarctic.

The Antarctic is land surrounded by water. The land is a desert. There are no plants. All the animals find their food in the ocean.

Look at the photos above. Which one is the Arctic? Which one is the Antarctic?

Glossary

desert – An area with very little rain or snow. It is very dry. There are few or no plants.

sphere – A round, ball-like shape.

tundra – A flat, cold region where no trees grow but grasses and small plants grow in the summer.

Reader 2 D LEVEL

Baby Birds

Foundations Level D Readers

Printed in the United States of America.

Royalty Free Images: Shutterstock

Logic of English, Inc
4865 19th Street NW, Suite 130
Rochester, MN 55901

ISBN 978-1-936706-17-4
First Edition
10 9 8 7 6 5 4

Denise Eide

www.LogicofEnglish.com

Duck hatching

Baby birds begin life in an egg. To get out of the egg, a baby bird must use its **hatching tooth**. A hatching tooth is a special bump on their beak used to break open the shell.

Duck hatching

They move the hatching tooth back and forth inside the shell until it cracks. Do you see the hatching tooth?

Duck hatchling

When a bird hatches, it is called a **hatchling**. Some hatchlings have feathers and can see from the time they are born.

Magpie hatchlings

Other hatchlings are bald. They have no feathers to keep them warm. Some hatchlings cannot see when they are born.

Guinea fowl protecting her chicks

Mother birds sit on the chicks to keep them warm. How many chicks is this mother bird sitting on?

Eurasian Eagle Owl

As a baby bird grows, it is called a **nestling**. Nestlings cannot fly. They are covered in soft, fluffy feathers called down.

Warbler nestlings

Nestlings are fed by their parents. When the mother bird is searching for food, the nestlings chirp.

Robin nestlings

When the mother returns, the nestlings open their mouths for the mother bird to drop in food.

Coppersmith Barbet

Some mothers bring fruit.

Robins

Some mothers bring worms.

American Oystercatchers

Some mothers bring crabs.

Garden Warbler

Some mothers bring bugs.

Eastern Bluebird

As the baby eats, it gets bigger and stronger. It grows long feathers that are used for flying. It begins to look like its parents.

Oriental White Stork

Baby birds that are ready to learn to fly are called **fledglings**. To fledge means to become ready to fly.

Great Tit

Fledglings practice flying by flapping their wings.

Osprey

It takes a lot of practice to learn to fly!

Pelican

Soon they can soar over land, lakes, and sea.

Glossary

hatching tooth – A special bump on the beak of a bird inside an egg used to break open the egg.

hatchling – A bird that has just hatched.

nestling – A baby bird that cannot fly, is fed by its parents, and still lives in the nest.

fledgling – A bird that is learning to fly.

Reader 3 D LEVEL

Bears, Bears, and More Bears

Foundations Level D Readers

Printed in the United States of America.

Royalty Free Images: Shutterstock

Logic of English, Inc
4865 19th Street NW, Suite 130
Rochester, MN 55901

ISBN 978-1-936706-17-4
First Edition
10 9 8 7 6 5 4

Denise Eide

www.LogicofEnglish.com

Sloth Bear

Sun Bear

Giant Panda Bear

Asian Black Bear

There are eight kinds of bears in the world. All bears are large, powerful animals.

Brown Bear

Polar Bear

American Black Bear

Spectacled Bear

Bears have a short tail and five toes on each foot. All bears can stand up on their back legs.

Sloth Bear

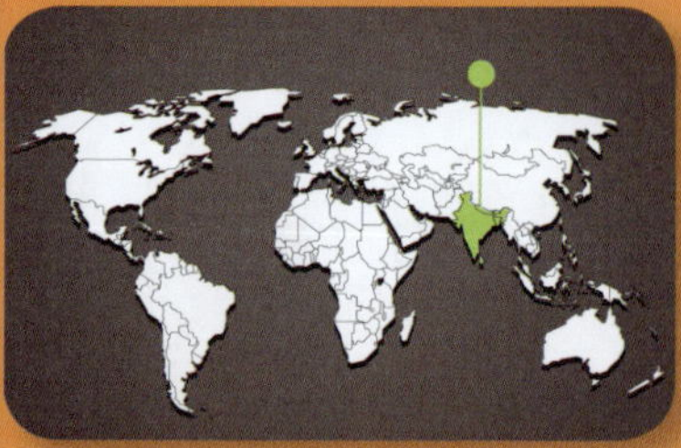

Sloth bears live in India, Bhutan, Nepal, Bangladesh, and Sri Lanka.

Sloth bears walk slowly. When sloth bears walk, their feet make a noisy, flapping sound. Sloth bears are good at climbing trees, and they like to hang upside down.

Termite nest

Termites

Sloth bears dig up termite nests with their long claws. Then they suck the termites through their long muzzle, which makes a loud gurgling noise.

Sun Bear

Cub

Sun bears live in southeast Asia.

Sun bears are the smallest of all the bears. They have long tongues to lick their food. Sun bears eat bugs and fruit. But their favorite foods are bees and honey.

Bee hive

Eating fruit

When a sun bear finds a bee hive in a tree, it destroys the tree with its strong claws to get the honey.

Polar Bear

Cub

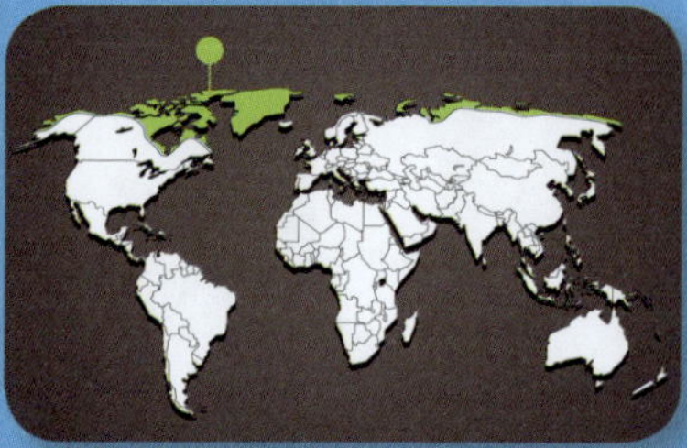

Polar bears live in the Arctic.

Polar bears live in the Arctic where it is cold. Polar bears have two layers of fur and four inches of fat called **blubber** to keep them warm. Having blubber is like wearing a warm coat.

Polar bears are good swimmers. They can swim ten days without stopping. Adult polar bears live alone. However, sometimes they meet to play together.

Brown Bear

Cub

Brown bears live in Europe, Asia, and North America.

Brown bears are very large. Some are ten feet tall. Brown bears are good at fishing. They stand in the water watching for fish to jump, then catch them in their mouths.

Brown bears use their long claws to dig dens where they can **hibernate** during the long winter. They sleep in a den all winter without waking up.

Giant Panda

Cub

Giant pandas live in China.

Giant pandas are **endangered**. There are only about two thousand pandas alive today. Pandas eat twenty to thirty pounds of bamboo every day. That is a lot of bamboo!

It takes them thirteen hours to eat that much! Pandas sleep up to ten hours a day. Between eating and sleeping, that leaves only one hour of extra time each day.

Asian Black Bear

Asian black bears live in China, Vietnam, Afghanistan, Pakistan, & Thailand.

Asian black bears are sometimes called moon bears, due to the white moon shape on their chest. They can walk upright for up to a quarter of a mile.

Asian bears that live in cold places hibernate from November until March in caves or hollow trees.

American Black Bear

American black bears live in North America.

American black bears can run up to 35 miles per hour. Black bears are also good at swimming and climbing.

In the summer black bears often sleep high up in tree branches. In the fall, black bears build a den in a cave or a hollow tree. When winter comes, they hibernate for up to five months.

Spectacled Bear

Spectacled bears live in South America.

Spectacled bears have white marks on their face that look like they are wearing glasses or **spectacles**. They are the only type of bear that lives in South America.

Spectacled bears are good at climbing trees and often build platforms in the trees to sleep in. Spectacled bears eat mostly plants and fruits found in the forest.

Glossary

blubber – body fat that keeps an animal warm

endangered – When an animal species has only a few left that are living. These animals are in danger of becoming extinct. If an animal is extinct, there is not a single one of that animal left alive on earth.

hibernate – to sleep through the winter without waking up

spectacles – glasses

Reader 4 D LEVEL

Carp
Unexpected Consequences

Foundations Level D Readers

Printed in the United States of America.

Royalty Free Images: Shutterstock

Logic of English, Inc
4865 19th Street NW, Suite 130
Rochester, MN 55901

ISBN 978-1-936706-17-4
First Edition
10 9 8 7 6 5 4

Denise Eide

www.LogicofEnglish.com

Goldfish

Koi

Silver Carp

Mirror Carp

The carp **family** is the largest family of fish with over 2,400 **species** (spē shēz).

All carp have some things in common. However, there are also differences between each of the species.

4 Carp

Pike with teeth on its jaw.

All carp have toothless jaws. Compare the carp's mouth to the pike's mouth. Notice the carp does not have teeth.

Many carp, but not all, have a **barbel** on each side of their mouth.

Carp

Notice the large scales on the body. Notice the lack of scales on the head.

Carp have large scales on their body. Often carp do not have scales on their head.

Rainbow Trout

A rainbow trout is not a carp. Notice the small scales.

Compare the scales of the carp to the rainbow trout.

Carp vary greatly in size by species. Some species of carp can grow to be very large, like this mirror carp.

Other species of carp stay so small they can be kept in fishbowls.

Goldfish are a species of carp commonly kept as pets. Goldfish can live in small spaces and in unclean water. This makes them easy to care for. Pet goldfish can live up to 40 years!

cowardlion / Shutterstock.com

Koi are another beautiful species of carp kept as pets. Koi are kept outdoors in ponds or water gardens. Koi are popular pets in Japan. In Japan, koi are a symbol of love and friendship.

Common carp are a favorite fish to eat in many parts of the world. For 2,000 years they have been farmed as food in China, Japan, and Europe (yer əp). Common carp can be farmed in ponds or kept in nets in lakes.

Common carp were brought to the United States and put in lakes and rivers as a good source of food. However, most Americans do not like to eat carp because it is oily and has lots of bones. Now common carp are crowding out the local fish in many lakes and rivers.

Aquatic plants

USGS photo - public domain

Grass carp

Grass carp were brought to the United States to control the growth of plants in lakes and rivers. However, no one knew that grass carp can eat as much as 32 pounds of plants every day!

Grass carp

In some lakes the grass carp ate all the plants. Other fish didn't have anything left to eat and began to die. Grass carp caused bigger problems than they solved.

Silver carp

Algae blooming on a lake

Silver carp were brought to the United States to clean the water by eating **algae** (ăl jē). Silver carp swim in large schools next to the surface. As they swim, they eat algae and filter the water.

Silver carp jumping

Silver carp are scared of boats. When boats drive along the water near them, the silver carp startle and jump out of the water. So many carp jump at one time that it can be difficult to enjoy riding in boats or fishing.

Carp are amazing fish! Some species such as the goldfish and Koi make great pets. Other species are a good source of food.

Learning about carp reminds us that it is not wise to bring animals from one part of the world to another. Sometimes there are unexpected consequences.

Glossary

algae (ăl jē) – A nonflowering plant. Most algae live in water.

barbel – A thin, whisker-like organ near the mouth of a fish. Fish use the barbel to taste the water as they search for food.

family – A group of animal species that have similar characteristics. Common animal families include dogs, cats, and bears.

species (spē shēz) – A group of animals of a specific kind that look similar to one another and can breed with one another.

Reader 5 D LEVEL

My Nest is Best!

Foundations Level D Readers

Printed in the United States of America.

Royalty Free Images: Shutterstock

Logic of English, Inc
4865 19th Street NW, Suite 130
Rochester, MN 55901

ISBN 978-1-936706-17-4
First Edition
10 9 8 7 6 5 4

Miriam Eide

www.LogicofEnglish.com

Birds must find a warm, safe place to raise their young. Each species has a favorite place to lay their eggs. As you read, guess what kind of bird builds each nest.

To build my nest, I scrape a small hole in the ground. This is called a scrape nest. My nest has very little lining. While I find food, the heat of the earth keeps my eggs warm.

I can swim well and so can my babies, so I build my nest by the water. When a **predator** is near, we can jump into the water and swim away.

My nest is best for ducks.

I live in the hot desert. To keep my eggs from baking in the hot sun, I build my nest underground. I use empty **burrows** that other animals have made.

I line the burrow with dung to attract insects. Then the babies do not need to leave the nest to have a tasty meal.

My nest is best for desert owls.

My nest is the most common kind of nest. I weave together grass and twigs into a cup. The eggs and babies are safe. They cannot fall out of the nest.

I build my nest in a tree, on a house, on a deck, or anywhere there is a flat space up high. Predators cannot reach us up here.

My nest is best for robins.

I weave my nest out of grass. It hangs upside down from a tree branch. The door is at the bottom. My nest looks like a grass sock.

It takes me eighteen days to build my nest. I like to be near the other birds, so I build my nest close to other nests.

My nest is best for baya weavers.

I make my nest out of mud. I scrape mud into a big mound with a bowl at the top. The bowl keeps the eggs from rolling out.

My nest is tall to keep water out. The mud keeps my eggs cool. I build my nest close to other nests.

My nest is best for flamingos.

I reuse the same nest for many years. Each year I add on to the nest. Each year my nest becomes taller and wider. One nest like mine was thirty-four years old before the tree fell down.

I build my nest up high so I can see my **prey**. Here my babies are also safe from predators.

My nest is best for eagles.

I carve my nest in the trunk of a tree. Other birds and animals often try to steal my nest. My nest is warm and safe.

I eat the bugs as they come into my nest from their homes in the tree.

My nest is best for woodpeckers.

I build my nest with other birds. Up to one hundred nests are all joined together to make one giant bird apartment complex! Each nest has its own entrance.

Our giant nest keeps the eggs cool. We help to raise each other's chicks. We are one big family.

Our nest is best for social weaver birds.

Each species of bird has its own style of nest. Which nest do you think is best?

Glossary

burrow – hole or tunnel in the ground made by an animal.

predator – an animal that hunts another animal for food.

prey – an animal that is hunted by another animal for food.

Reader 6 D LEVEL

Frog or Toad?

Foundations Level D Readers

Printed in the United States of America.

Royalty Free Images: Shutterstock

Logic of English, Inc
4865 19th Street NW, Suite 130
Rochester, MN 55901

ISBN 978-1-936706-17-4
First Edition
10 9 8 7 6 5 4

Miriam Eide

www.LogicofEnglish.com

Many people do not know that all toads are frogs. But be careful! Not all frogs are toads.

Life in the Water

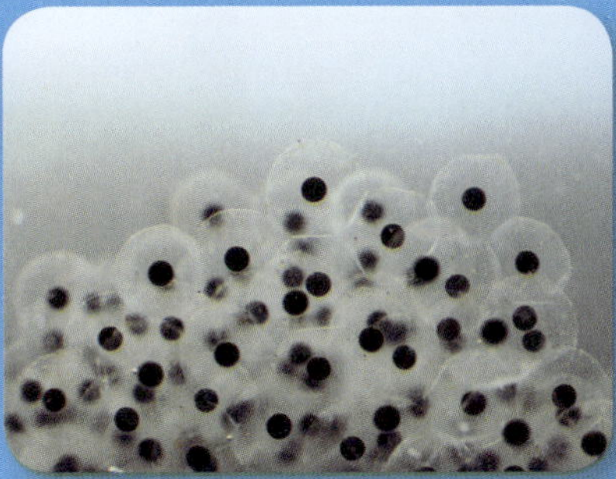
Eggs

Tadpoles

Life on Land

Adults

All frogs are amphibians. *Amphi* means both and *bian* comes from the root *bio*, which means life. Amphibians live both on water and on land. They spend part of their life in each environment.

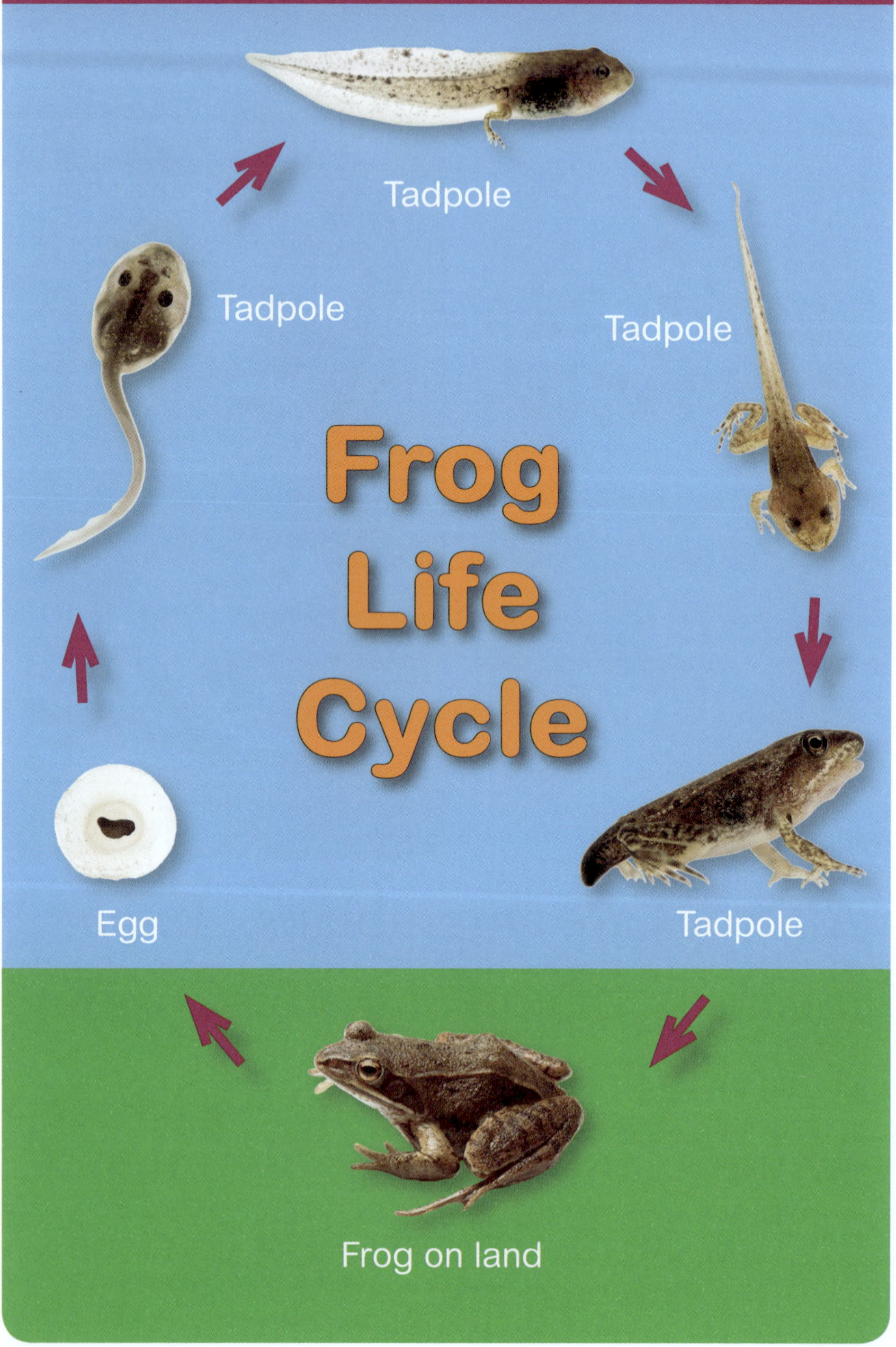
Tadpole
Tadpole
Tadpole
Frog
Life
Cycle
Egg
Tadpole
Frog on land

A tadpole changing into a frog

All amphibians begin life in the water as eggs. When frog eggs hatch, they become tadpoles. Like fish, tadpoles breathe water through **gills**. Over the next twelve weeks the tadpoles will grow legs and lose their tails and gills. Soon they will begin their second life on land as frogs.

All frogs, including toads, have ears behind their eyes. A frog's ear is called a **tympanum**.

Toad

Frog

Frogs do not have necks. Therefore frogs' eyes bulge out so they can see **predators** and **prey**.

Frog

All frogs have tongues attached at the front of their mouths. This allows frogs to flick out their tongues a long distance to catch prey. All frogs swallow their prey by pulling their eyes down onto the roofs of their mouths.

All frogs eat insects, worms, slugs, and other small animals.

Frog

Toad

Frogs that are not toads are called true frogs. Toads have a number of differences from true frogs.

Toads have short legs. Toads hop short distances.

True frogs have long legs. True frogs jump long distances.

Toads can live away from bodies of water for long periods of time.

True frogs must live near water.

True frogs have smooth, moist skin. True frogs breathe through their skin. They will suffocate if their skin becomes too dry.

Toads have rough, bumpy skin. Because toads have lungs like humans, a toad's skin can dry out without suffocating the toad.

Sac with poison

Toads are poisonous to eat. To protect themselves against danger, toads may also puff up so that they look big. Toads use **camouflage**, which helps to hide them from **predators**.

Most true frogs are not poisonous to eat. These frogs depend on puffing up or playing dead for survival. Most true frogs also use camouflage.

Looking at the pictures, can you decide which ones are true frogs and which ones are toads?

Glossary

camouflage – coloring on an animal that hides it or helps it blend in with its surroundings.

gills – the organ that fish and tadpoles use to breathe in water.

predator – an animal that hunts or preys on another animal.

prey – an animal that is hunted by another animal for food.

tympanum – a frog's ear.

Reader 7 D LEVEL

Many Kinds of Feet

Foundations Level D Readers

Printed in the United States of America.

Royalty Free Images: Shutterstock

Logic of English, Inc
4865 19th Street NW, Suite 130
Rochester, MN 55901

ISBN 978-1-936706-17-4
First Edition
10 9 8 7 6 5 4

Denise Eide

www.LogicofEnglish.com

Different types of animals have different types of feet. Animals' feet are specially **adapted** to help them live in particular habitats, catch their prey, and get away from their predators.

My feet are adapted for life in the water. I have feet with three connected toes. Feet with connected toes are called **webbed** feet. Webbed feet help me to swim fast. I find much of my food in the water. I can use my feet to walk on land. But I cannot perch in a tree like other birds.

What am I?

I am a duck!

My feet are adapted for life in the Arctic. My front feet have webs between the toes to help me swim fast. I have big pads to keep me from slipping on the ice, and fur to keep my feet warm. I have long, sharp claws that I use to make snow caves and to catch my **prey**.

What am I?

I am a polar bear!

My feet are adapted for living in trees. I have three toes on each foot. My toes are long and orange. Each toe has a suction cup. The suction cups help me to grip onto plants, trees, and leaves.

What am I?

I am a tree frog!

My feet are adapted for walking and running long distances. I have thick round hooves that protect my feet from getting sore. My hooves are made of the same stuff as your fingernails. Sometimes I wear metal shoes to protect my hooves. The shoes are hammered on with nails. It does not hurt.

What am I?

I am a horse!

My feet are adapted for living in trees and hunting prey. My feet have three claws in front and one claw in back. Each claw ends in a long nail called a **talon**. I swoop through the sky and grab my prey with my feet. My toes curl around the prey and grip it tight.

What am I?

I am an eagle!

My feet are adapted for life in the forest. I have hooves with two toes. My toes help me balance on uneven ground. They help me run fast to get away from danger. My hooves are sharp. If I feel threatened, I can use them to kick my enemy.

What am I?

I am a deer!

My feet are adapted for carrying a heavy weight. I walk on my toes. I have heavy padding on the bottom of my feet. My feet are sensitive. I can feel animals approaching or a storm coming. My feet do not leave foot prints, so I am difficult to track.

What am I?

I am an elephant!

My feet are adapted for running fast! I can run up to 43 miles per hour. My feet flex to help me balance on uneven ground. I have only two toes. I also use my strong legs and large claw to defend myself. With one powerful kick I can kill a **predator**.

What am I?

I am an ostrich!

Glossary

adapt – to change in a way that helps an animal live and thrive in a particular habitat

habitat – a place an animal lives, including the plants, soil, climate, other animals, etc.

predator – an animal that hunts another animal for food

prey – an animal that is hunted by another animal for food

talon – the claw on a bird of prey

webbed – having connected toes

Reader 8 D LEVEL

Mouse and Mole

Foundations Level D Readers

Printed in the United States of America.

Royalty Free Images: Shutterstock

Logic of English, Inc
4865 19th Street NW, Suite 130
Rochester, MN 55901

ISBN 978-1-936706-17-4
First Edition
10 9 8 7 6 5 4

Miriam Eide

www.LogicofEnglish.com

Mice and moles are different from one another. They have different habits and appearances. To begin with, mice usually live above ground.

Moles, on the other hand, live in tunnels below ground.

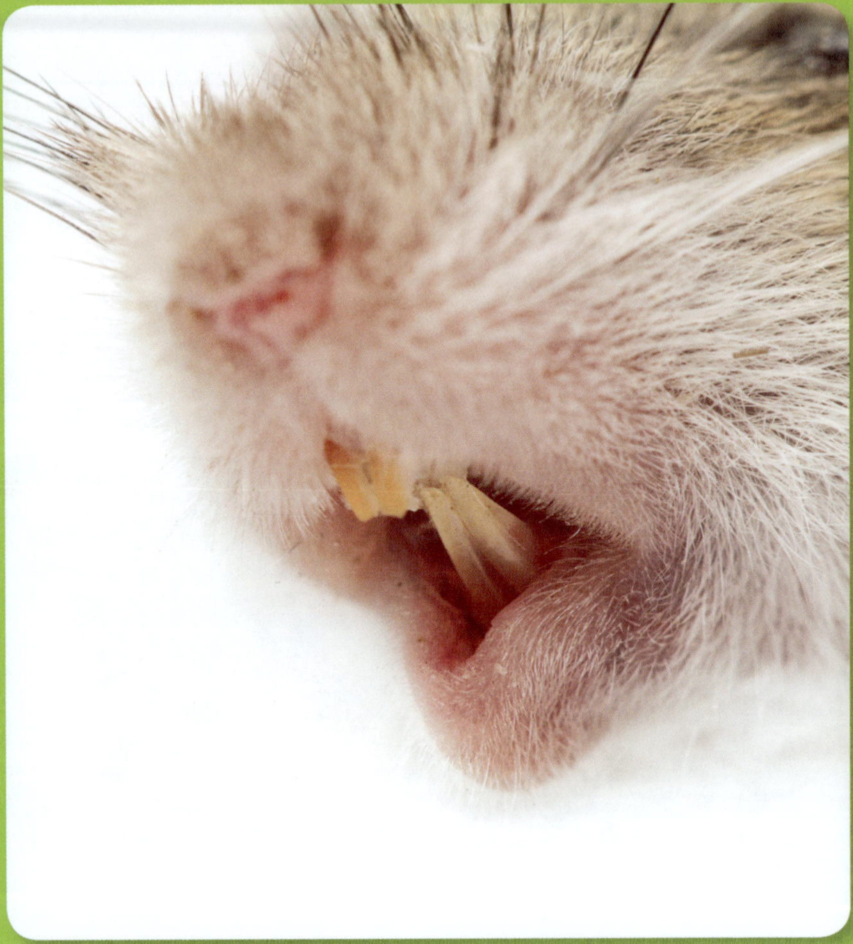

Mice have four front teeth that grow continuously. They wear down their teeth by chewing.

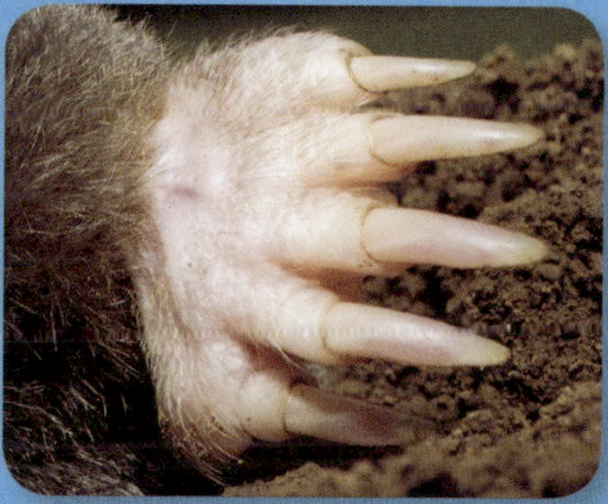

Moles have tiny teeth. They have large front paws with long claws for digging.

Mice have little feet. They build nests in trees, in holes, and sometimes in houses.

Moles live in networks of tunnels, which are always expanding. They can dig as many as twenty meters of new tunnels in a single day.

Mice are usually **herbivores**. An herbivore eats only plants. Mice prefer to eat grain, seeds, berries, and other plants.

Moles are **insectivores**.
Insectivores eat insects and
worms.

Mice eat fifteen to twenty small meals a day! A mouse eats about one seventh of its body weight each day.

Moles eat whenever they are awake. They will starve in eight hours if they don't eat. A mole eats half its body weight every day!

Day

Night

Mice are **nocturnal**. Nocturnal means that they sleep all day and are awake all night.

Moles sleep and wake in four hour cycles. They are awake for four hours, and then they sleep for four hours.

Mice can see well. They also use their whiskers to sense their surroundings.

Moles are almost blind. To get around, moles feel what is around them with their whiskers, noses, and fur. Moles also have good hearing and a good sense of smell.

The body of a mouse is about three inches long. Mice have thin, long tails. Mice weigh only one ounce.

The body of a mole is about six inches long. Moles have short tails. Moles weigh about two ounces.

Mouse fur lies all in the same direction. Look at the picture. Notice how all the fur points back. Mice have **external** ears that stick up above the mouse's head.

Moles have fur that can lie forward or backward. Moles have **internal** ears. This way their ears do not get caught in their tunnels.

Mice and moles are very different!

Glossary

insectivore - an animal that eats insects and worms

herbivore - an animal that eats plants

nocturnal - asleep during the day and awake at night

external - on the outside

internal - on the inside